Praise for *Stop and Frisk* by Jabari Asim

"Urgency and imagination, truth and focus: Jabari Asim brings those qualities together in a book of poetry that confronts the lethal face of racism: death-by-police. This book challenges the boundaries of the art by being, in a very good sense of the word, *documentary*."

—Robert Pinsky

"These poems read like a play of our lives composed of recognizable voices, but in Asim's finely wrought *Stop and Frisk*, we are newly compelled to hear. Beyond the pain, he manages to lift beauty to the surface, the beauty we forget about in the midst of a struggle. There has never been a time when the keen eye of Jabari Asim has been more necessary."

—A. Van Jordan, author of *The Cineaste*

STOP AND FRISK

American Poems

Jabari Asim

BLOOMSDAY

Published in the United States by Bloomsday Literary
bloomsdayliterary.com
Houston, Texas

No part of this book may be reproduced, in any form, without written permission from the publisher.

If you would like to use material from the book (other than for review purposes), prior written

permission must be obtained by contacting the publisher. Request for permission should be e-mailed

to info@bloomsdayliterary.com.

ISBN 978-0-9998239-4-1
Library of Congress Control Number: 2020932470
Printed in the United States of America
FIRST EDITION

"Pinch Me" previously appeared in *The American Poetry Review*.
"The Talk" previously appeared in *The Washington Post*.

Book design by Houston Creative Space

For all the Erics, Eleanors, Renishas...

STOP

AND

FRISK

# CONTENTS

## 1

## 3

Now will the poets sing,—
Their cries go thundering
Like blood and tears
Into the nation's ears,
Like lightning dart
Into the nation's heart.

—Countee Cullen

1

# Young Americans

Dead children make mad noise
when they march, sounding their frustrated yawps
over the rooftops of Chicago. Neither wind nor monstrous
guns can stop their stomping.

       Dead children make mad noise
       when they march. The doomed, solemn-eyed youth
       of Chicago are putting boots on the ground,
       gathering in ghostly numbers
       to haunt us with their disappointment.
       It's hard to miss them swelling the Water Tower crowds
       at rush hour, clogging Cottage Grove inconveniently,
       taking up all the seats on the El.
       The Dan Ryan is stop and go
       from all the phantom overflow as they troop
       through the city's arteries.
       South Side, West Side, all around the town.

Battered and battle-hardened,
the spirits of collateral children rise up
armed with experience, the worst kind of knowing.
The spirits of collateral children drip blood
across the big-shouldered city, spattering
the landscape like poppies dotting Flanders Field,
looking for someone, anyone, to take up their quarrel.
They high-step in rhythm, according to a cadence
only they can hear:
Hup! Two! Three! Four! Through that hog butcher history,
Sandburg's singing niggers, Capone's cutthroats,
bullets falling like fat rain on a street in Bronzeville.

       The slaughtered innocents of Chicago,
       young Americans who loved and were loved,
       are braving the crossfire

of hand-wringing and corruption,
the photo-friendly choirs
and drive-by eulogies, politicians'
cue-card declarations of sorrow.

The slaughtered innocents of Chicago
ain't going nowhere gently.
Circling the sad metropolis
in loud, unearthly ranks,
they raise their voices to the bloody sky,
above the roar of the monstrous guns and the
bullets, falling like fat rain.

# So You Think You Can Dance?

Me and rhythm tight as Ronnie, Bobby, Ricky, and Mike
turning and sliding in one smooth move,
telling a packed house of screaming girls to Cool It Now.
My father always going on about New Edition,
Ralph's street-slick falsetto and Johnny G's rumbling like
a natural man. I just tell him, Pop, it hurts me to say it,
but New Edition is Old Edition now. Bobby barely moving
these days, looking like he needs a hip replacement, and
not a single one of them feeling stupid enough to try a split.

Me and my boy Andrew know all the ancient history.
Pop say, you can't break the rules unless you know them, so
when we not dancing we on YouTube, checking out the tradition.
Early mornings we Get On Up like the Godfather of Soul,
stretching and soaking up MJ popping that crazy robot
in Dancing Machine, his brothers'
shrink-proof Afros bobbing behind him.
The Temps, neck-tied and double-breasted,
showing Young America they Ain't Too Proud To Beg,
the Nicholas Brothers taking folks to school,
Jumpin' Jive.

We got all that in our bones by the time we reach
First Avenue, leap up and ask the straphangers
to clear the middle.
Not much room to moonwalk on the A Train,
so I take to the air.
We're formally trained, Andrew explains,
both graduates of the MTA academy, where
we majored in rhythm and minored in flight.
I'm upside down quick as a Knick, curling my ankles around
the chrome and letting my body say what words can't.

Tourists whip out iPhones while others look through us
like we clear as the air they hope will swallow us up
as we pass through the populous city.
I know those types: sooner or later
the rhythm is gonna get 'em.
Andrew hasn't even passed the hat
before four plain clothes pop up and
place us under arrest. The foreigners think
it's part of the show as they turn and slide
us through the doors.

# The Talk

It's more than time we had that talk
about what to say and where to walk,
how to act and how to strive,
how to be upright and stay alive.
How to live and learn,
how to dig and be dug in return.

When to concede and when to risk,
how to handle stop and frisk:
Keep your hands where they can see
and don't reach for your ID
until they request it quite clearly.
Speak to them politely and answer them sincerely.
The law varies according to where you are,
whether you're traveling by foot or driving a car.
It won't help to be black and proud,
nor will you be safer in a crowd.
Keeping your speech calm and restrained,
ask if in fact you're being detained.
If the answer is no, you're free to go.
If the answer is yes, remained unfazed
to avoid being choked, shot, or tazed.
Give every cop your ear, but none your wit;
don't tempt them to fold, spindle, mutilate, hit
or otherwise cause pain
to tendons, bones, muscles, brain.
These are things you need to know
if you want to safely come and go.
But still there is no guarantee
that you will make it home to me.
Despite all our care and labor,
you might frighten a cop or neighbor
whose gun sends you to endless sleep,
proving life's unfair and talk is cheap.

## Pinch Me

Call me constable
on patrol,
Leopold carving up the Congo
into three blocks of
crumbling corners
and foreclosures unfolding
into imperial turf.
My space:
No Mexicans, Assholes,
or Ex-Ho's allowed.

I am what makes you a man
in my book,
hollow points in my pocket
and nine millimeters hard against my hip.

Then he lurks,
lean and lion-like
leering and loitering
for the 46th time, growing taller
as I approach.

I'm the hunter so I'll get to tell the story
of my valiant defense.
Already I'm putting words in his mouth,
my stubborn brownness glowing
in the whites of his eyes.
Aside from his scream
it's a breathless affair
as I offer him up
to the god of crackers and concrete.

My head how it throbs
The rush of blood
The rush of blood
The rush

# Vanishing Point

SOCIAL WORKER
Six weeks a no-show
before anyone raises alarm.
Her mother says she's sick,
under a doctor's care.
No note, no nothing, to explain
where Relisha went.

Red tape is every bureaucrat's burden,
even one who cares enough to leave
her pile of reports and look into
how a young girl apparently ceased to exist.
Follow a trail of evictions, garbage,
cigarette butts, cut lips, insults,
infections, and defections.
Trace her tiny footsteps to a shelter
where raccoons in the closets have the roomiest
rooms and lurking custodians flex tattoos.
It takes paperwork and paperwork,
permissions, procedures, and approvals
to approximate the touch of a hand.

What she may have left behind:
a numb mom and three hungry brothers,
dirt, scabs, bedbugs, and a teddy bear
named Baby.
One photo breaks my heart.
She is facing the camera,
peeping through a pipe cleaner
twisted into a circle not quite complete,
like a wound that will not close.

MR. TATTOO

I've been thinking sameness is a sin.
Day in, day out, dirty mop water, high blood pressure
and the same woman beside you for twenty-four years.
Technically I'm the janitor but I was made for so much more.
God meant for me to have beauty, bright and brand-new
every day. What is more bright and beautiful than a little girl?
I'll tell you: three hundred of them
at the DC General shelter, where I can keep them happy
with a fistful of twenties and quarters for the candy machine.
You can catch more kids with sugar, just like flies.

Don't nobody care about these kids.
Half they mamas don't want 'em
and the city sure don't.
They can't see the shine they give off
like Baby Girl, with her braids and barrettes,
eyelashes a grown woman would die for.
Day by day I'm feeding her dreams,
presents, talking to her teddy bear
while she listens and laughs.

I wear the ankh on my arm
because I'm committed for life.
The tattoo keeps 'em curious,
convinced I've got the key to happiness.
I used to be Karl, now I'm Kahlil,
born again and a big man on the yard.
Renamed and renewed,
I rock the polos, suits, and ties
to match the sparkle of my tuned-up SUV.
Baby Girl and me, we're gonna get up from here
and hit the road.
You'll see her for the last time at Holiday Inn,

pink boots and paper bags streaming light
from a security camera.
Meantime, ladies get so they look forward to me coming around,
sweeping floors, fixing flooded toilets, whistling sweet tunes.
How does that song go?
Hey girls, gather 'round, I'm your handyman.


RELISHA
He take me to the movies.
He take me to the mall.
He give one girl a turtle tank
but my mama say don't fret.
Just turn on that smile and he'll be back,
jingling change.
He bring me a lollipop
for all the birthdays before
he knew me,
tells me I don't have to share.
The best sweets, he say, don't belong to nobody but you.

2

# Cancer Sold Separately

In the South End we saw a man throw a tantrum
outside the walk-up window of a gas station,
yelling, sputtering, and shaking. No, not shaking; dancing.
Dancing like Samuel L. Jackson in *Jungle Fever*, cajoling
cash from his heartbroken mom.

"Let me get a loosie! Damn, a loosie, man! Let me
get one! A loosie!"

Apparently he'd slept on the surgeon general's warning
to black men: bellowing in public
may be hazardous to your health.
He was probably too young to remember when
Winstons tasted good like a cigarette should.
Shelves were lined with Kents, Viceroys, Tareytons,
Salems, Kools, Pall Malls, Lucky Strikes, Marlboros,
Belairs—all the brands an eight-year-old could fetch
from the corner confectionary without a sleepy shopkeeper
blinking an eye.

We had helpful jingles then. Now
we've lost track of God's infinite variety
of flavorful carcinogens.

Our man didn't care about any of that. He just wanted
a single cigarette. One goddamn loosie.
His voice was rough-edged and ashy.
A cough coiled in his chest, waiting to spring.
The Asian clerk, his eyes on the end of a long shift,
could have been a statue.
"Damn! You speak English?"
Maybe. Probably. But he definitely spoke Unimpressed.
He shrugged and looked beyond the loudmouth
to the next person in line.

Dissed and dismissed, mocked by the gods,
the black man went operatic, weepy,
a luckless sucker in a street corner farce.
Cursing his fate and the dumbass clerk,
insisting on his right to die a little bit at a time,
he pounded on the reinforced glass
as if he could thrust right through
and choke him out.

# The Disappeared

Every portrait posted on the Black and Missing website
looks like someone I know,
last seen in parking lots and on porches, at work,
leaving church, heading to class, rolling cross-country
to visit friends. Sixty-four thousand
mostly missing in New York, Georgia,
North Carolina, Maryland, and Florida:
signs of struggle, prints wiped clean,
empty cars with engines running.

So many women, so little news.

All these Americans the thin air has swallowed,
no Chandras, Caylees, or Natalees among them.
Phoenix, Shani, Arnika, Sharaun, Tilawna, Latoria,
how your smiles stay with us,
your winning gleam.

In Chile, the mothers and wives of the disappeared
would dance in protest at the government gates.
How shall we announce our scars and fractures,
our sustained despair?
I dream of a drumbeat summit,
millions of men stepping and sliding in electric syncopation,
a train of souls whirling beyond the White House fence.

# Because I'm Happy

My man Pharrell says the new black
knows that beefing is beneath him,
that blaming other folks for your problems
ain't nothin' but a thang. The new black,
he says, has to choose which side he's on.
It's all about your mentality
changing your reality.
I'm happy to hear it,
happy as a room full of room
as I head for the Staten Island streets.
My wife's kiss has me high
as a hot air balloon.

Back in the day I treated every cop like a suspect,
waiting to mess with me every time he saw my face.
I expected bad news and grieved for things I'd yet to lose.
It may sound crazy what I'm about to say:
I'm tired of it; it stops today. I'm the new black now,
so give me all you got and don't hold back
because can't nothing bring me down.

# Loosies

On certain street corners a man can scare
up a cigarette for just one dollar.
Enough loosies over time can be hazardous to health,
as deadly as breaking up a fight in an intersection crowded
with witnesses or dashing through drizzle for Skittles and tea.
Risks aside, they are a staple of urban commerce, a gross
domestic product that helps the underground economy go.
Picture Boy Willie and his watermelons,
Bearden's bejeweled fishmongers
bartering amid a splash of paint.

But a black man in the middle
of the night knows better than
looking for loosies beyond his own driveway.
Safer instead to root around the glovebox
for that precious, planned-ahead pack.

Later he'd say it felt like a firing squad
when deputies opened up from behind, leaving him
not only smokeless but sixty years old and shot in the leg.
Suspected of stealing his own car in front of his own house,
he thought his neighbor was joking when he heard a
command to put his hands in the air.

3

## Warning: Contains Graphic Violence

Attention all units,
black woman walking
eastbound on I-10
near the La Brea on-ramp.

Approximately 5′ 5″ tall, 135 pounds,
early fifties,
answers to Grandma.
Wearing a pink dress and appears to be armed
with a purse.

If you encounter the suspect,
she may resist by walking slowly away.
Throw her on her back and squeeze her
between your thighs.
Raise your fist high and punch her face
until she is still. She may resist by
continuing to breathe, in which case
raise your fist high and continue
to punch—one two three four five
six seven times. Is she still moving?
Punch her again.
Again.
Again.

Be advised that this is a high-risk pursuit.

# Menace to Society

Attention all units,
black woman walking
outside the lines
near College and 5th.

Approximately 5' 4" tall,
early thirties,
answers to "Professor."
She may resist by flexing her vocabulary,
insisting on respect and kicking your shin.
At that point, consider your life in danger.

Be advised that promising to slam her
conforms to university police protocol,
as does twisting her arm behind her back
before you throw her to the ground.

Cuff her quickly, taking whatever liberties
necessary to keep Arizona clean.

# Where the Party At

I
I wake up forgetful.
My head is pounding at sunrise,
before sunrise even, when the world is still quiet
and dreams still cling.
Finally gold seeps softly through my curtain and I know
what's outside my window without getting up to look.
Mr. Craig is walking his dog. Mrs. Williams is filling her feeder
with seeds. The only sound is the Purnells'
sprinkler tisk-tisking over grass neat and green
as the home team's outfield.
I might have thought of softball or spring.


LONZO
I wake up with watermelon and cherry
all up in my grill like bits of broken glass.
Candy, bitches, and Kool-Aid—I like
everything sweet.

Man-Man must be crazy
to call sizzurp and sandwiches a party.
A few tens up in the crib but we talking
mostly fives and sixes. Had my eye
on that quiet girl with the braids but
Man-Man was being Man-Man,
boxing me out like LeBron in the paint.
I'm like Man, it's me, Lonzo.
He ain't trying to hear me.

So. What. Plenty of fish in the sea.
I do what I do: talk shit, act like I'm high,
and let the music get me lost.
When the party was over I crashed on his couch
chewing Jolly Ranchers till I fell asleep.

MAN-MAN

I was just gon' chill, for real,
maybe catch the game or whup
Lonzo's ass on Xbox, but my niggas
go texting, talking about where the party at.
Moms is working a double so
I say come on through
while I hit up some ho's.

II

A secret soreness makes its way,

swells in me,
a dream that clings.
A party, noise,
faces from school.
I can almost remember.

He must have put something in my drink.
It hurts to think.

LONZO

Want to stop them Jews and them
from killing each other?
Hook up a drone and drop Jolly Ranchers
all over that joint.
Bomb them motherfuckers with flavor, feel me?

I want to tell the girl with the braids about it
while the fellas slurp that sizzurp.
Man-Man say shut up fool but he don't know everything.

    MAN-MAN
    I put a little something in her cup.
    Trick-ass bitch drank it right up.

III
Ringtones erupt and I see myself on the screen,
naked, outside of time.
I'm either asleep or the scene of the crime.
The soreness grows. My body
reminds me.

On Twitter he calls me everything
but a child of god.

    LONZO
    Man-Man, hold up,
    I say to him.
    Man-Man, hold up,
    but he ain't trying to hear me.


The fellas get out their cells.
I turn away.
I don't do nothin'
but turn away.

She a sweet girl too, I could tell.
Sweet, like I like 'em.

MAN-MAN
Don't listen to Lonzo.
He just pissed
that I scored and he swung
and missed. If that girl didn't want to party
she should have stayed home.

IV

Memory clings
but it's a dream that I want,
before everything breaks
into hurt, noise, and ever after.
In the dream I'll be faceless with no name,
dissolving in soft green spring,
birdsong, and morning's embrace,
awash in gold.

## don't start none

you got one more time,
I told him. one more
time to get in my face,
to call me out my name.

there you go again, he said,
softer now. just quit playing
and stop starting shit.

by then it was too late,
the gun rising in my hand
as if it was alive.

aw, you supposed to be
bad now, he said smiling.
it was a nasty smile,
the kind you flash when there's
nothing between the two
of you but the goodness
you can't stand to lose.
he grinning like that even
with his little boys standing
right there. the oldest one
trying to tell me something
but I ain't got time for it,
not just then.

don't start none won't be none
was the thought in my head
when the gun went off
loud as any words I could shout,
the oldest boy shutting his eyes,
the little one shaking
and covering his ears.

all I hit was air. the silence
afterward stole our breath
before he grabbed the boys
and stumbled, a man out of time
staring back at the me he'd never seen,
a woman wreathed in smoke,
standing her ground.

# A House Is Not

Man up, little man.
Walk it off.
Our father would say those words whenever
my brother or I stubbed a toe,
bumped our heads, got thrown to the floor
in the fearful tumult of our house.
It was a lesson he learned in Little League,
he said. The coach would pelt a boy with
batting practice fastballs until he learned not to flinch.
It's only a ball, just a ball, and if a pitch catches you
in the ribs, flip your bat, hitch your pants,
spit, and jog toward first until the heat subsides.

Many a baby mama had learned
to face his screwball velocity and take it on the chin,
including our own mother.
When his latest wife stepped to the plate
I tried to help her.
Walk it off, I warned,
it's only a fist, just a fist.
But she shook off the signs
and raised her gun.

Man up, I said to my brother,
When the gun went off above our heads.

# Wild Things

Two minutes half-naked in the company of at least a dozen men with guns does things to your mind each minute becomes a thousand years you think of headlines and history your great-grandmother raped by white men with guns on the dirt floor of a barn what she remembered most were those who stood and watched, doing nothing while the horses turned away in shame and disgust men with guns men smelling of sweat and desperation pounding on my door I tried to close it but they were too strong a dozen men against one woman yanked into a hallway of noise nightmare lights screaming cops and yelling neighbors my towel tugged away leaving me in underpants a scrap of fabric between me and the grasping hands of strangers my bare body pushed and pressed into the cold and unforgiving wall begging to be let go praying for mercy and darkness to hide my dark naked self from the eyes of strange men with guns looking me up and down as they go up and down the stairs not one man handing me my towel to cover my breasts married for sixteen years and ten went by before my husband saw all of me my oxygen beyond reach the space tight as the hold of a ship eyes hands breath mean men pressing against me squeezing while the good men watch a neighbor shouts y'all wicked as the four-year-old goes down in a cloud of spray one man's sour breath on my neck hard against my back his fingers in my mouth men with many eyes hands taking up my air neighbors in the stairwell with cameras say I fainted and fell to the floor the good men stood all around all around the good men stood all around

4

# Check the Manual

With a knee in his back
and a heel on his head,
he remembers Officer Friendly.

The first-grade visit from the precinct's Community
Outreach ambassador was his first face-to-face
with a cop. Until then he'd known them only
as a pair of bullies who terrorized his neighborhood,
sending the big boys scrambling at the sight of their cruiser.
Of all the kids he could have chosen to help with his presentation,
the officer, black and smiling, singled him out.
In front of the class, including his secret loves Linda and Lori,
he laughed shyly and presented his wrists for cuffing.
While Officer Friendly read him his rights,
he risked his bookish reserve for a taste of swagger.
It went down smooth as Kool-Aid, put fire in his bones.
Was Linda grinning? Did Lori sigh and shift in her seat?
Behaving as a bad guy was cool and contagious.
Now he sees it was just practice, dress rehearsal as the iron
bites his wrists, a hundred hammers pummeling him
into the pavement.

Last week in the barbershop, old heads and young
talked of prisons and pipelines,
of shaping souls from birth for shackles and cells.
His mama raised no fools but it was still too big for belief—
simply talk, conspiracy theory, urban legend, a joke
of Def Comedy proportions. How did
Richard Pryor put it?

*Can you break a nigger? Is it okay?*
*Let's check the manual.*
*Yup, page 8.*

He'd laugh if not for the loose teeth,
the gravel in his throat.

# False Confession

Can a nigga get a drink of water?
It's hot as hell up in here.
What you mean I should be used to the heat?
Nigga, I was born in the dead of winter
and my people been in the north since shorty was a pup.
Been in this country longer than you and yours, you leprechaun lickin'
potato famine refugee.
Yeah, I know your story, I heard it in in school. What the fuck you know about
     mine?
Detective, better check your boy.
He eyeballin' me hard, all up under my clothes
like he never seen a pretty muthafucka before.
Yeah, me and my boys was in the park. Yeah, we seen her.
We was there poppin' wheelies and spittin' game at bitches. But nobody hollered
     at her because she could use a sandwich and we like 'em thick.
Besides, I ain't never had to take what's freely given.
Talkin' shit ain't rapin' nobody last I heard, unless y'all done gone and
     changed the rules again. It's hard for a nigga to keep up.
Too close for comfort, son, back up a bit. No offense, but your breath is kickin'.
Tic Tacs and Scope should come with the job along with a gun and a badge.
Fuck a chokehold, you can just *breathe* on a nigga. Can we open up
     a window?
What's up with my phone call? My mama's back from work by now and
     wondering
where I am. Is the water fountain broke? Y'all didn't pay the water bill? Lookin'
     at a nigga get thirsty and doin' nothin' about it is cruel and unusual, yo.
I'm sweatin' because it's hot as fuck, not because I'm nervous.
For real, though, detective, your boy is making me a bit jumpy,
lookin' at me with that spit dripping out the corner of his mouth.
Hey what the fuck nigga get your fingers out my locks! I don't know where your
     hands been—well, I did see you feelin' up them schoolgirls in the park
     just before you jumped
me and my boys. What did y'all do with my bike?
Damn, nigga, stop pulling my hair. That's right you bad, my worst nightmare

you say

but you don't even know what a nightmare is.

Yeah that's right keep talkin'.

Another time, another place, nigga drop your white ass before you know
what hit you.

What the fuck you got me chained to a fuckin' table, what you scared of you so
bad? Let me loose say that shit and see how long you live.

Lawyer, son, how many times I gotta say that?

I know my rights. I'm sixteen and I been here before. You ain't tryin' ta hear me.

Lawyerlawyerlawyerlawyerlawyerlawyerlawyerlawyerlawyer.

Yo, behind the glass! You gettin' this shit on tape, right?

Back up off me, son, for real.

# Found Poem #1

For what?
For what?
For what?
Because I'm sleeping?
Ain't no relax.
Somebody record this.
Stop playing with me alright?
For what?
I didn't do shit.
This is bullshit.
I'm sleeping.
Record all of this please.
Record all of this.
I'm going back home.
Stop playing with me.
I didn't do shit.
I'm sleeping.
What are you doing?
What the fuck is he doing?
All this for what?
Yo! *You* making it worse!
I didn't do shit.
For what, for sleeping?
There's clearly bums on the train that sleep.
I'm coming from *work*.
I'm coming from *work*.
You don't need to arrest me.
You don't need to arrest me.
For what? For what?

Y'all fuck with me for no reason.
Write all this down.
Get off me!
No! No!
Keep hittin' me!
Keep recordin'!
Get off me!
See this?
You see this.
All this for what?

**Mehserle** [MEZZ-er-lee]: *verb* 1. to shoot an unarmed civilian in the back at close range, often when civilian is handcuffed or otherwise subdued, usually in front of a crowd 2. To serve less than a year in prison after shooting an unarmed civilian in the back at close range

*Word history*: A criminal court jury convicted BART transit police officer Johannes Mehserle of involuntary manslaughter in 2010 and acquitted him of murder. He was released in 2011.

*Example*: "I figured he'd pull a Mehserle and get out next month. Then I learned he'd kicked a puppy so he'll be in for a while."

**Pantaleo** [PAN-ta-LAY-o]: *verb* to strip, humiliate, choke, detain without cause or otherwise abuse an American citizen in a public setting, often in front of witnesses

*Word history*: In 2013, two black men sued NYPD officer Daniel Pantaleo for violating their civil rights, including strip-searching them in broad daylight, handcuffing them, and searching their genital areas. Each man received a $15,000 settlement from the city. Pantaleo is the same man seen applying a chokehold on Eric Garner, an unarmed citizen, in a widely distributed cell phone video.

*Example*: "Dude, they Pantaleo'd his ass in front of the whole neighborhood."

**Volpe** [VOL-pee]: *verb* 1. To torture, sodomize, assault or otherwise abuse a handcuffed civilian, often as a result of mistaken identity 2. To abuse a civilian and attempt to cover it up

*Word history*: NYPD officer Justin Volpe rammed a broken broomstick up Abner Louima's rectum on August 9, 1997, and attributed his severe injuries to abnormal homosexual activity.

*Example*: "That wasn't the first time five-o pulled a Volpe on a brother. It was just the first time they got caught."

# Found Poem #2

If Mr. Walking Heart Attack
had simply put his hamburger shovels behind his back,
he wouldn't have had a heart attack.

All he had to do was comply and he would not be dead.
Tough shit and too damn bad.

# One thousand chokeholds from now

black and brown people will cross at the corners.
They will refrain from heaving rocks at panes of glass
and stop grilling meat on the sidewalks.

One thousand chokeholds from now,
they will stop dancing in subways.
They will decline to sell individual untaxed cigarettes.
They will not climb from car wrecks to seek assistance.
They will not resist arrest by holding on to the hems of their skirts.

One thousand chokeholds from now,
black and brown people will no longer insist on access to taxis.
They will not step into elevators when white women are already inside.
They will wait patiently at Best Buy when a snot nose kid checks
and double-checks their receipts.

One thousand chokeholds from now,
windows will not be broken and neither will heads.
Cities will be clean and safe
for lovers of local lager, artisanal pickles,
and the hipsters Nextdoor.

One thousand chokeholds from now,
James Q. Wilson won't be nothing
but the name of an endowed chair at the American Enterprise Institute,
paid for by State Farm, because like a good neighbor
they are always there.

## Furtive Movements

eleanor bumpurs tyisha miller anthony baez
jonathan Ferrell claude reese amadoU diallo
miChael wayne clarK jonny gammage
oscar granT moHammed assassa seAn bell
central Park five latanya haggerty henry dumas
sOnji taylor jordan davis johnny robinson
eula Love michael stewart rekia boyd
prince jamel gavIn eliberto saldana aiyana jones
marCillus miller rodnEy king abner louima
kenneth chamberlain sr. julio nunez
patrick dorismond jimmie lee jackson

# Barney Fife Gets Totally Lost

Looks like we took the wrong ramp
and got ourselves plum turned around.
You burned that curve like Otis on a bender;

likely you were drunk on Aunt Bea's chicken basket
and cherry pie. Sure, I'll get out and have a look-see,
no trouble a-tall. One bullet in my pocket

in case of emergency means if I run into trouble
I'll nip it. Nip it in the bud.
It's good sometimes to get out

from under and breathe the urban air,
get a taste of city life. Yonder
I see homeboys, just like I pictured them.

I'll approach those fine gentlemen for directions,
swap homespun philosophies and tips on
the care and feeding of firearms. Then

we'll be back to Mayberry in a jiffy.
I'll bet Juanita is keeping a seat warm
for me at the Junction Café.

I tell you, Andy, small-town love brings
nothing but heartaches.
Wouldn't you agree?

Andy?

# Found Poem #3

Don't resist. I don't understand why these people don't simply comply.

I guess it's the best thing for his tribe. He probably never worked a legit job. The city will pay off the family and they will be in Nigggaaa heaven for the rest of their lives!!

If the fat fuk just put his hands behind his back none of this would have escalated into what it did.

Tell Deblowzio to get his azz to Italy.

Stop. Let me see ~~your hands.~~
You ~~in a hurry?~~
Where you rushing off to?
~~Yeah?~~ You live around here?
Let's see some ~~ID.~~
~~I ask the questions.~~
~~I ask the questions, you~~ shut the fuck up
~~and do what I say.~~
ID!
~~Don't make this hard.~~
Fuck the constitution,
~~take a knee. Take a~~ goddamn ~~knee.~~
Still talking? ~~You still talking?~~
Got him? ~~Okay, okay, press~~
~~his head down. Danny, J,~~
pin that sucker's legs.
Put the boot on him. ~~That's it.~~
Cuff him. ~~Oh was that~~
~~your arm? My bad.~~
Who's the badass now?
~~You like that?~~
You like that ~~fucking concrete, tough guy?~~
~~You want a~~ baton ~~up your ass?~~
~~Ask you to do one simple thing,~~
you go and assault a police officer.
~~You have the right to~~ remain silent.
~~You have the right to a~~ broken ~~jaw.~~
~~You have the right to~~ choke ~~to death.~~
~~You have the right—Yo!~~
~~Kill that camera or~~ you're next.

5

# We Steal Weaves
*after Gwendolyn Brooks*

    Caught on video.
        Four at Mr. Indian Hair Supply.

We steal weaves. We
bold thieves. We

real ill. We
got skill. We

talk slick. We
move quick. We

still fail. We
in jail.

# Memorials, Jersey City

Two T-shirts taped on a wall,
flanked by heart-shaped balloons.
Defiance and peculiar cheer.
Below them, bottles emptied
for the homies who ain't here.

The sentiments on the shirts,
scrawled by passers-by,
remind Lawrence Campbell he was loved,
and real niggaz don't die.
He'll live on in legend
for gunning down police:
La La. Big Bro. Thug In Peace.

–

Outside Walgreens,
a pair of portraits of the victim
in uniform dress.
Columnar candles arrayed in a line
beneath a blood-red sign:
"Video Recording in Progress."

Bouquets huddle in sorrow,
bitter to behold.
A hand-made sign reminds us
that the righteous are bold.

Officer Melvin Santiago,
just twenty-three and newly begun,
hadn't even drawn his gun.

# Action Figure

shit being Strange everywhere makes shit here no less Strange than say,
Sun Ra singing Strange celestial roads, Strange as young black men strangling

themselves in the backs of cop cars while handcuffed and lying face down, Strange as
navel lint passing for poetic introspection, Strange as Strange young citizens, sons

and daughters of dick-pic Democrats and retrofitted Republicans, all a-Twitter over
America's hottest convict: desperate Strangers getting Strangely choked

up over a black and blue-eyed felon in his orange jumpsuit (the face that launched a
thousand clicks), a Strange obsession briefly broken when Strangely colorful

action figures bearing his Strange plastic likeness were Strangely stifled as soon as they
were Strangely introduced. the struggle to keep this Strangeness stoked.

6

# Affluenza, or Judge Jean Boyd Earns Her Silver Gavel

CHARACTERS

Ethan Couch

Scott Brown, Texas defense attorney

G. Dick Miller, defense psychologist

Judge Jean Boyd


THE DEAD

Hollie Boyles, 52

Shelby Boyles, 21

Brian Jennings, 43

Breanna Mitchell, 24


ETHAN

So we stole some beer from Walmart

and went out in search of joy.

Happiness is hard to come by

when you're a poor little rich boy.

I didn't mean to hurt anyone.

I screwed up, okay?

But that doesn't mean I can't turn things around.

Why should I do time when my daddy can pay?


THE DEAD

(Silence)


SCOTT BROWN

What Ethan needed was structure and love.

What he got was stuff.

He feels terrible about what he's done.

Your Honor, isn't that enough?

THE DEAD

(Silence)


G. DICK MILLER

Your Honor, privilege is a sickness
like affluenza, insidious and real.
Only therapy, not jail,
will help our victim heal.


ETHAN

Once I got caught with a girl in my car,
naked, unconscious, and only fourteen.
Mom and Dad can get me out of anything
and keep my hands clean.
I'm sorry, dammit. Can I go now?
Look, my family will do whatever it takes
to help me see the error of my ways
and atone for my mistakes.


JUDGE JEAN BOYD

When it comes to self-improvement,
prisoners often fail,
so I'm sending you to therapy
and keeping you out of jail.
After two years of treatment
you'll be over your disease
and your parents will be waiting
with their checkbook and your keys.


THE DEAD

(Silence)

# The Kind That Scares You

I am black and staggerly,
dark-knuckled and nappy.
Seeing me walk the streets
made much of Florida unhappy.

I'm the ghost of your criminal past,
your easy alibi.
I'm black and poor in Florida,
where Justice goes to die.

Accused of seven robberies,
I denied them all.
They say I fired a weapon
but they saw nobody fall.

Tell the judge I'm underprivileged;
I need therapy instead.
I'm bipolar, after all,
and no one's hurt or dead.

Way down south in Dixie
(Break the heart of me)
Poor boys go to jail,
Rich boys go free.

# Thug Life

What up, shorty?
Get closer, let me holler.
I see you peeping my pinstripes, my cufflinks and my collar—
like Erick and Parrish I'm making mad dollars.
You a dime piece, girl, top of the shelf.
Let me buy you a drink and introduce myself:
Undergrad Harvard, MBA Tuck.
Pleased to meet you, it's just my luck
to discover you so lovely in your little black dress,
such a sexy match for my American Express.
I'm an investment banker, an original gangster,
a VIP, and this world is mine.
The sucker MCs have to stand in line,
waiting for the bus while I drive my Bentley.
Am I living right? Evidently.

Sucker MCs get hired to haul trash;
I spend my days conjuring cash
and stock accumulation,
CDOs, creative obligations,
mergers, closings, and liquidations.
As banks go, so goes the nation:
assembly-line losers getting shown the door,
the rich getting richer off the sweat of the poor—
it ain't no secret what democracy is for.
My portfolio's loaded, and I'm ready to roar.

Suckers lose their houses while the mad world spins.
Banks reap rewards for a multitude of sins.
People call for trials but that ship has sailed...

(Never been arrested for nothing domestic.)

...homeboys getting choked but the banks are getting bailed.
Best of all, ain't nobody getting jailed
like Milken and Madoff.
Suckers in factories getting laid off
and losing their pensions,
clowning in school when they should have paid attention.
"No snitching" is the stitching on every baller's label—
hell, I've even got it tatted 'round my navel.
Listen up, turned up, it's time you learned up:
Mortgage Fraud Task Force is a joke in your town.
One percent up, ninety-nine down.
I'm rocking white power in its whitest hour
yet my ambition is extensive.
I'm looking for a soulmate who's thirsty and expensive
and admires my swagger.
I exalt single-malt but you'll never see me stagger.
I won't render unto Caesar except maybe a dagger.
Taxes are played out, Glass-Steagall's toothless,
and we're working day and night to keep the government useless.
We got an army of lobbyists advancing our cause,
slipping cheddar in the pockets of the men who write the laws.

(Why do I want to be a congressman
when I can own Congress, man.)

Our crew comes correct, working on the Hill,
advising legislators while they write the bill.
Then they come back to the Street and feel no pain,
rocking a corner office and making it rain.

(Circle of life, you feel me?)

How about it, sweetness, can I get you alone?
Like two turntables and a microphone,
I'm built for pleasure and bad to the bone.
Money can't buy love but it can buy a nice crib.
Penthouse, private entrance, that's how I live.
Carrara marble, mahogany floors,
rooftop garden through the sliding doors.
Beluga by the scoop, steak by the stack—
once you love a thug you know you'll never go back.
Room by room, I'll walk you through it.
I'm a banker for life and this is how we do it.

7

# CNN Sends a Man to Ferguson

*after Gwendolyn Brooks*

In Ferguson the people raise
their hands above their heads and praise
God, his works, and his mysterious ways.
They ask for justice before peace
and pray for suffering to cease.

Nighttime brings danger and caprice,
wayward men in tanks, lawless police.

In Ferguson, the people earn their bread
to keep their children fed
and a sheltering roof overhead.

They drive home with care
to avoid a policeman's baleful stare
and the siren's dreadful blare.

I broadcast
and folks lean in
to absorb my clever spin,
my glossy lips, my chiseled chin.
Behind me, history marches past.

In Ferguson is hiphop; heavy bass.
That rhythm of summer…rhymes, fury, grace
born of a particular time and place.
Battling the heat, clawing the troubling dust.

There is love, too, in Ferguson, softness
and hardness and grateful receiving.
Out of anguish a resilient weaving
of heart and flesh and breath,
a respite from riotous, impudent death.

In Ferguson they know
the world prefers to turn away,
ignoring the forces of corruption at play
in a little town making a killing
from tickets, fines, and occasional blood-spilling.

I had blamed their circumstance
on absent fathers and sagging pants.
But after two days here I can see
why the revolution won't be on TV.
I wonder as I wander among these Vines, streaming loops,
and Twitterbugs scrambling for scoops
(I'd scratch my head but I'd muss my hair.)
how to get this sound bite on the air:
People in Ferguson are like people everywhere.

(An Emmy? A Peabody? I imagine accolades
between the tear gas and shock grenades.)

It's true, some are talking trash
and urging others to plunder and smash.
But amid the artillery and armored thugs who curse and shove
I've seen mostly peaceful people acting out of love.
In days to come, arguments and retorts,

double-talking cops and missing incident reports.

Live at five: I remind the world why we're watching this town.

His name was Michael Brown.

# Walking While Black

*for Michael Brown*

A man walking in the middle of the road.
A man walking in the middle.
A man walking.
A man.

Walking in the middle a man.

A car rolling down the middle of the road.
A car rolling down the middle.
A car.
Rolling.

Walking in the middle,
a man.

Heat rising in the middle of the road.
Heat rising in the middle.
Heat.
Rising.

A cop in the middle of the road.
Cop in the middle.
In the middle of the road a cop.

Man, heat, and cop in the middle of the road.
Man, heat, and cop in the middle.
Man, heat, and cop.
Man.
Heat.
Cop.

In the middle, Man. Heat. Cop.
ManHeatCop.
ManHeatCop

A gun firing in the middle of the road.

                     –

A man running in the middle of the road.
Running.
A man.

A gun firing.
A gun.

Firing.
Firing.
Firing.
Firing.
Firing.
Firing.
Firing.
Firing.
Firing.
Firing.

In the middle of the road.

A man falling in the middle of the road.
A man falling in the middle.
A man
falling.
A man.

A man dying in the middle of the road.
A man dying in the middle.
A man.
Dying.

Heat.

# Reckoning

*for Renisha McBride*

1.

Mournful horns right here
      Deep thrum of bass

Mournful horns right here
      Deep thrum of bass

2.

A stone's throw from Motown,
Hitsville, USA.
      The sound of America eating its young.

3.

Renisha reeling,
head full of fire,     wreck and
ruin behind her.

4.

Theodore Wafer, 55.
Home alone
with a shotgun
and a cell
phone.

5.

I thought they would hurt me. I thought I could scare them off.
Theytheytheytheythey. They.

6.
Under age.
Under the influence.
Nineteen.

Wafer investigates.
Through a locked
screen.

7.
He sees nothing but night.

8.
I would not cower in the face of this awful blackness this dark
mistake this sable error this dusky neck too distant to strangle
but close enough to shoot I would not cower I would not.

9.
Swing the bottom electric.
Lighten the brass, for a few beats.
Step it up some. One of them Junior Walker joints,
a burst of inappropriate funk.

Shotgun. Shoot 'im 'fore he runs now.

10.
Full of piss and vinegar, I unlocked my door
          and stepped outside.

11.

white humor white Christmas white comedy white lies white out white
lines white cloud white tornado white lightning white privilege white rights

He has her in his sights.

12.

No more odes for the Confederate dead.
Let's grieve for Renisha instead,
all the Renishas, the broken sisters crushed to dust
and bone in our neighbors' tangled pathologies. Weep for their sparkling
promise, their incandescent love.

13.

Mossberg. Pistol grip.

14.

His tragic story of accidents

                                    suddenly changes to self-defense.

15.

Nothing that night went the way he planned.

                           Wafer

wipes a tear on the stand.

16.

Horns, more mourning.
Come on in and blow now if you want to,
we're through.

Wreck and ruin.

Deep thrum of bass.

# Notes

15. In recent years, Chicago's gun violence murder rate has surpassed New York's, despite the latter having three times as many people. The violence has hit children especially hard. In 2012, for example, 443 people were shot dead in Chicago, with 65 of them being 18 or younger (*New York Daily News*).

17. "Subway dancers have unwittingly found themselves a top priority for the New York Police Department..." (*The New York Times*, July 28, 2014).

22. "District's police chief says Relisha Rudd most likely dead as search turns into recovery" (headline taken from *The Washington Post*, March 27, 2014).

35. On July 1, 2014, onlookers used a cellphone camera to record an unidentified California highway patrolman pummeling Marlene Pinnock, 51, as he straddled her near an on-ramp in Los Angeles. The beating has been viewed around the world.

36. In May 2014, a campus policeman threw Ersula Ore to the ground while arresting her for jaywalking. Ore, a professor at Arizona State University, was sentenced to nine months probation for resisting arrest.

44. "Denise Stewart, 48, opened her Brownsville apartment door to NYPD officers, who heard shouting coming from inside the home, police said. When Stewart, who was wearing only a towel, tried to close the door, cops yanked her into the hallway" (*New York Daily News*, August 1, 2014).

51. According to the NYPD, the man was originally targeted for "committing a Transit Rules and Regulations violation of laying outstretched occupying more than one seat" (*New York Magazine*, July 3, 2014).

54. Language taken from comments posted on NYPD internet discussion forums (*New York Magazine*, July 21, 2014).

55. Of the 1,022 chokehold complaints New York's Civilian Complaint Review Board has received since 2009, only 10 have resulted in a recommendation of serious discipline from the board. "In each completed case, the police commissioner at the time, Raymond W. Kelly, opted for a lesser punishment or no punishment" (*The New York Times*, August 5, 2014).

58. Language taken from comments posted on NYPD internet discussion forums (*New York Magazine*, July 21, 2014).

69. Sixteen-year-old Ethan Couch, driving drunk and speeding, plowed into four people standing on the side of a road. All four were killed.

71. The line "Way down south in Dixie" is taken from "Song for a Dark Girl" by Langston Hughes. In 2014, Quartavious Davis was sentenced to 1,941 months—almost 162 years—in prison without the possibility of parole. No one was hurt or injured in his alleged offenses (*New York Daily News*, July 4, 2012).

79. A police officer in Ferguson, Missouri, fatally shot Michael Brown, 18, on August 9, 2014. Brown, unarmed, was walking down the middle of the road with a friend.

82. On August 7, 2014, Theodore Wafer was found guilty of second-degree murder, manslaughter, and felony firearm charges for the death of 19-year-old Renisha McBride. Wafer claimed he shot her on November 2, 2013, because he thought she was an intruder. She was seeking help after a car accident.

# Also by Jabari Asim

NONFICTION

*Not Guilty: Twelve Black Men Speak Out on the Law, Justice, and Life* (editor)
*The N Word: Who Can Say It, Who Shouldn't, and Why*
*What Obama Means: For Our Culture, Our Politics, Our Future*
*We Can't Breathe: On Black Lives, White Lies, and the Art of Survival*

FICTION

*A Taste of Honey: Stories*
*Only the Strong: An American Novel*

CHILDREN'S

*The Road to Freedom*
*Whose Toes Are Those?*
*Whose Knees Are These?*
*Daddy Goes to Work*
*Girl of Mine*
*Boy of Mine*
*Fifty Cents and a Dream*
*Preaching to the Chickens*
*A Child's Introduction to African-American History*
*My Baby Loves Christmas*

POETRY

*Sing It Like a God: American Poems*

The text of *Stop and Frisk* is set in Edita, designed by Pilar Cano, a Barcelona-based typeface designer.

Cover and book design by Houston Creative Space

# About the Author

Jabari Asim is the recipient of a Guggenheim Fellowship in Creative Arts and the author of seven books for adults—including *We Can't Breathe: On Black Lives, White Lies, and the Art of Survival*—and ten books for children. His poems are included in several anthologies, including *Furious Flower: African American Poetry from the Black Arts Movement to the Present*; *Beyond the Frontier: African American Poetry for the 21st Century*; and *Role Call: A Generational Anthology of Social & Political Black Literature & Art*. After more than a decade at the *St. Louis Post-Dispatch* and *The Washington Post*, he now directs the MFA program at Emerson College.

CPSIA information can be obtained
at www.ICGtesting.com
Printed in the USA
LVHW051726240720
661451LV00005B/723